Dr. Cunningham

FOCUS ON YOUR FOCUS!

Unexpected Expectations:

Motivation vs Inspiration

Volume 1

*An Interactive Guide To Getting The
Best From Your Life And The People In It.*

Based on the research, education and expertise of

Dr. LaJeanna L. Cunningham

PEN PUBLISHING AGENCY

Pen Publishing Agency | Lafayette, Louisiana

Unexpected Expectations: Motivation vs Inspiration

Published by PEN Publishing Agency
Lafayette, La 70508
2020, 2020 by Dr. LaJeanna L. Cunningham

Published 2020
First edition published 2020
Printed in the United States of America
www.penpublishingagency.com

Dedication

I dedicate this book to my son – my ever present teacher.

As well, I want to thank the "2020 BABs."
Your advice, candor and general acceptance of me mattered!

This page intentionally left blank

Table of Contents

Purpose

*"You can look for external sources of motivation and that can catalyze a change, but it won't sustain one. It has to be from an internal desire." - **Jillian Michaels***

This book, which is the first in the Unexpected Expectations series, is intended for adults and professionals to better understand their roles in generating desired outcomes. The contents of this book are my real life scenarios and the application of my own research as well as the research of others. I utilized this combination to explain the critical differences between motivation and inspiration. Why do you need to know that? "… knowing how to leverage what makes them distinct can lead to a better chance of achieving long-term successful outcomes for your team" (Popomarouis, 2019). Understanding the roles of motivation and inspiration will ultimately save you time and money as you manage your life and the people in it.

Introduction

Why "Unexpected Expectations"? If we take a critical look at the world and people around us, we'll learn that others hold expectations of us that we may or may not be aware of. Something as simple as crossing the street comes with seemingly obvious expectations of a pedestrian and a driver. Yet, in 2017, 5,977 pedestrians were killed in traffic crashes in the United States. That equates to roughly one death every 88 minutes. Per trip, pedestrians are 1.5 times more likely than passenger vehicle occupants to be killed in a car crash (Rosen and Sander, 2019).

When we know what is expected of us we know what to do. When we are unaware of expectations, things can get messy. This series is intended to share insight on some of life's unexpected expectations so that you become reminded to look both ways before crossing the street.

> *"Real obsession needs an unconscious motivation behind it." - **Damon Galgut***

Who am I to tell you about motivation, inspiration and why you should care? Professionally, I am Dr. LaJeanna Cunningham. Owner and Chief Learning Officer of The Learning Firm, LLC, The PHX Foundation (a 501C-3 organization) and "Dr. Cunningham" - collectively called 'the legacy' (look that up at www.llcunningham.com). For the last 20 years, I have worked directly or contractually with employees and leaders of some of the largest organizations. My fascination with human behavior led to earning a doctorate in Human Performance Improvement.

Personally speaking, I am a woman and a mother. A mother to one. A mother to seven. A mother to an entire community of young males. I held my son Carter, for the first time when he was just three weeks old. He's 19 years old now and I've yet to put him down.

Motherhood was never on my to-do list. At 14, I aspired to be a high powered corporate woman who wore expensive suits and drove an expensive car. One who worked well past 5pm at her desk and ate Chinese food out of the container with chopsticks. I was intrinsically motivated to be a high achiever. Thus far, I've accomplished a unique version of that. It's has been a journey!

Instructional Dynamics was the first company that I started. It was a consulting firm specializing in training, learning, development and change management. I was awarded three contracts and was earning a salary of $70,000 annually. Two years into owning my company, talks of separation began between my ex-husband and I. By the time the actual separation happened, a recession hit and the first thing that companies cut from their budget was training and development.

Unexpectedly, I found myself unemployed, living in an apartment that I couldn't afford while living on cash advances from credit cards.

Coincidentally, there was no alimony nor child support from my ex-husband but let's not focus on the unsupportive cast members just yet. To make a long story short, I was now a single mother with a school aged child, living on my own with no family or friends to help. Despite my current status, I was armed with my faith and a Master's degree. I was motivated to become forever self-sufficient.

Chapter 1: Motivation

"The success of our efforts depends not so much on the efforts themselves, but rather on our motive for doing them." —Denis Waitley

Merriam-Webster defines motivation as having an incentive to do well or succeed in some pursuit (Merriam-Webster's Collegiate Dictionary, 2020). Motivation is an internal push to do something. Often we hear people, leaders, in particular, say they want to motivate someone. An example of this is a father wanting to motivate his son to play on the school team. A wife wants to motivate her husband to spend quality time with her. The pastor wants to motivate his parishioners to volunteer. A corporate leader wants to motivate their staff to meet quarterly goals. At some point in our lives, we all want to motivate someone to do something.

Did you notice in the examples above, Person A aspires to motivate Person B to do what Person A wants? The question becomes, "How?" Can one person create an internal push in someone else? Especially if Person B doesn't know how to do the thing, doesn't know to do the thing, or (and, this is most often the case) doesn't want to do the thing. The answer is one person cannot motivate another. I heard you gasp. Let me explain.

Carter was always the student that one teacher appreciated but the next would label as disruptive – for the exact same behaviors. I tried several ways of managing Carter's behavior through motivation. My goal was to support the teacher and help my son learn without altering who he was. I tried rewarding, disciplining and ignoring in an attempt to obtain the desired behaviors. During the year of the separation, one of Carter's teachers labeled his advanced ability to reason and communicate as disruptive.

Having moved from a diverse community to a predominately white community, for the first time, Carter found himself to be the first and only Black person in the room. Familiar with his behavioral history in the classroom, I knew that I would need to stay in tune with him to differentiate between him "just being Carter," him truly being disruptive, and his being Black.

During this time, I was also the most financially challenged. Because Carter was just a child, he didn't realize that we were eating mostly sandwiches and not going to the movies as much. It was easy to say, "Let's walk to the store for exercise," when I didn't have enough gas to get to the store and back. This also segued into why we couldn't buy a lot of groceries because we couldn't carry a lot.

He didn't notice the shift from drinking soda, juices, and Gatorade to just drinking water "… because this is healthier for us." He still had a video console and games that kept him distracted at night. So, he didn't hear me in my closet, crying and praying. He didn't hear me, asking for forgiveness for whatever I'd done to deserve this life.

13

He also missed the one male visitor's coming and going. The one who brought groceries or gas money in exchange for "my time." His innocence shielded him from my struggle.

We moved immediately after his third-grade year. So, Carter and I spent our first summer without the pressures of school. Carter, being the social butterfly he is, made friends quickly. I found comfort in that. Knowing that I'd added "my parents are divorcing and I don't see my dad anymore" to Carter's emotional and mental self, I anticipated genuine acting out during the new school year, his fourth-grade year.

About the third week of school, I planned to preempt the undesired behaviors at school by introducing rewards not for doing well but for not misbehaving. "Carter, if we get through the week without any issues, we'll go get a happy meal. We'll go to the McDonald's that has the big indoor playground." This was one of his favorite things to do.

My strategies to inspire my son to behave well worked! The teacher and I agreed there was some noticeable effort to do well that week, but there had been a few minor issues. The compromise was that we'd still go to McDonald's but not the one with the playground. I'd deposited yet another cash advance check. So, we went grocery shopping first and then headed to McDonald's!

We pulled up to the drive-thru and placed our order. Carter gave me his version of school events, which, oddly, I always understood. My role was to help him understand the teacher's perspective and how he's not wrong, but he's not right either.

We pulled up to the first window, and I handed the cashier my debit card. He swiped the card and gave it back to me. Carter's and my conversation moved to Beyblades, the latest fascinating toy. He saw another one he wanted. Apparently, it lit up differently than the other 15 he already had. I immediately saw this as a carrot to motivate him to get through the next week without school issues. "Moms. Always a step ahead." Feel free to tweet that.

This page intentionally left blank

Chapter 2: Inspiration

*"The most important thing is to try and inspire people so that they can be great in whatever they want to do." - **Kobe Bryant***

The word inspiration sounds spiritual and uplifting. Merriam-Webster defines inspire as a spurring on to exert an enlivening or exalting influence (Merriam-Webster's Collegiate Dictionary, 2020). To inspire means to influence. Consider these examples. "After listening to the speaker, I was inspired to write a book, finally!" Watching the documentary inspired me to renew my gym membership. Hearing how my father ultimately died from alcoholism, I was inspired to stop drinking. Notice in these examples, the person was affected by an outside influence to do something they wanted to do. Can one person inspire another? Let's find out.

So, we left off with Carter and I in the McDonald's drive-thru, and I'd paid for his happy meal at the first window.

Well, when we get to the second window, the McDonald's employee told me my card had been declined. And, they'd already run it twice. I'd only ordered his happy meal. The total bill was $4.45. I didn't argue with the employee but told Carter there must be a mistake. I pulled up to an ATM to try to withdraw cash. I was unable to do so. I requested a summary and saw that my account was at a negative number. I was confused more than embarrassed because I'd just deposited that cash advance check. I told Carter I needed to go home to call the bank to find out what happened. He said, "It's ok, Mom. I'll just have a sandwich." He didn't say it disappointingly. He stated it as a solution. Still not understanding the situation, I just said, "OK" and drove home.

A few calls later, I learned that the credit card company declined the cash advance due to my credit history. The pending amount covered the grocery bill at the time. But that would later be added to the negative balance. As would the charge from the gas station. The check I wrote for the rent would eventually bounce. At the end of that day, I had no money and no income.

I was a 38-year-old woman with a master's degree, in America, with no source of income - including alimony and child support - and a small child. I could not afford to buy my only child a $5 happy meal. Damn.

I'd struggled, financially, before, but never with a child in tow. Carter had no one but me. Literally. Again, I could go into the lack of support from the supporting cast members, but it's irrelevant to the story. That night, I laid prostrate on the floor and cried. And, cried. And, cried. I thought of who I could call – and what those calls would costs. And I had the harsh awakening that not only did Carter have no one but me but I, also had no one but me.

QUESTION 1: I've developed a firm goal to become forever self-sufficient. Do you think I was motivated or inspired by this situation to achieve my goal?

☐ Motivated   ☐ Inspired

Let's continue.

I allowed myself that night to cry and feel sorry for myself. But I knew my strength and my credentials and knew this situation was temporary. It had to be. It simply had to be. I knew what I had to do for a long term solution. I had to apply for jobs I was over qualified for. Even if that meant being a cashier somewhere. I had to get over "… but I have a Master's degree" and focus on survival. I was in a financially dire situation. Facing that truth, I also had to face what I needed to do for a short term solution. I called him. Again. And, I had to make that call a few more times before I gained employment.

QUESTION 2: Do you think I was motivated to call and ask for help? Or was I inspired by the potential of financial help?

☐ Motivated　　☐ Inspired

I would say that 'focus on survival' and 'financially dire situation' are motivators. These were internal dynamics that no one gave me. These motivators are what drove my short term and long term solutions. Again, no one had to coerce me to do anything.

I was a single mother who was financially destitute. I was motivated as hell. Someone I connected with while working on one of my contracts saw my resume and hired me at $40,000 per year. Obviously, the salary was less than what I wanted, but it was income. Let's take a pulse check.

QUESTION 3: Do you think:

- I was motivated to accept a job for less money, or

- The hiring manager inspired me to accept a lower paying job?

I see your wheels turning. And, you're correct. Had this job offer come along when I was still employed and making $70k per year, there's no way I would have accepted it. So, the hiring manager did not motivate me. Not being able to buy my son a happy meal motivated me to accept a job paying almost half of what I was expecting.

Since I knew the inner workings of this company, I knew how to position myself for bonuses and promotions. But was I motivated by the potential promotions? No. 'Focus on survival' and 'financially dire situation' were my motivators. I was inspired to be an exemplary employee to address my motivators – not my manager's will or the organization's goals.

Chapter 3: Why It Matters

"Leadership is not about a title or a designation. It's about impact, influence and inspiration. Impact involves getting results, influence is about spreading the passion you have for your work, and you have to inspire team-mates and customers." -
Robin S. Sharma

Research from the American Psychological Association reveals that finding meaning in one's work is ultimately a far more significant predictor of engagement, satisfaction, career growth, and decreased absenteeism than any other factor. This was even true of "undesirable" industries, such as sanitation (Weir, 2013). Understanding the difference between motivation (an internal drive) and inspiration (an external drive) will help you understand how to address the people in your life (ex: children, partner, staff) in a meaningful and productive way. When you understand that you're dealing with a lack of motivation or a lack of inspiration, you'll know where to focus your energy and resources. Um-hm, you're welcome.

So, the new job was within a reasonable distance and came with health insurance but required I spend 50% of my time traveling out of state. I would only have to travel to Houston but might need to stay up to two weeks each time. I would stay at the Embassy Suites, have a rental car and a daily stipend for meals. I looked forward to the break of providing for myself every day. All I had to do was get up and go to work. The rest would take care of itself. But, what about Carter? Again, my support system in Richmond was next to none. Obviously, the first option for extended child care was my ex-husband. The man whose last name Carter still has. The first trip was a three-day trip. When I picked Carter up, my ex-husband informed me he could not keep Carter again. He understood that I didn't have family or close friends to leave Carter with. But his having to get Carter to and from school and then care for him in the evenings interfered with his work schedule.

And, something, something, something. And, blah, blah, blah.

A few months passed before I had to travel again. By this time, I'd made a few acquaintances at work. The next two trips were about five days each and, each time, I left Carter with co-workers that I was comfortable with but had known for less than a year. It was less than ideal but driven by my motivation to be forever self-sufficient; I remembered why I was inspired to take this job. This was a part of it, so I resolved to trust God and my instincts.

My coworkers had not lived on 'a nice' side of town but had the desire to. Understanding there was the motivation or a hook, as a colleague calls it. Instead of offering money, I offered a five-day stay in my gated apartment complex. With their stay at my apartment came access to all the amenities to keep Carter at no charge to me. Did I motivate them to babysit? Nope. I inspired them. They were motivated by their desire to 'live' in a nice neighborhood with pools, a mall within walking distance and no imminent danger. I, now, have friends who are living 'higher on the hog' than I was then. They would look at me with muffled laughs if I'd made them the same offer. I'm reminded of when Donald Trump won the 2016 election and refused to downgrade and move into the White House. Heehee. It's all about perspective. And, a person's perspective creates their motivation. An external force cannot create motivation. It can inspire. But it cannot motivate.

Another quick example is the threat of pending homelessness. I know a person who was homeless as a child and has a genuine fear of being homeless again. He worked alongside someone who was currently living in their car. Their manager, having seen the quarterly goals were missed, again, came into the shop and barked, "If you two don't meet these goals within 30 days, one of you will be fired!" Did the manager motivate or inspire either of them to change their performance?

QUESTION 4: Which one do you think adjusted their performance? And, why?

Homeless as a child? Why?

_____

_____

Currently homeless? Why?

_____

_____

This page intentionally left blank

Chapter 4: So, Now What?

"Life is but a collection of consequences from our decisions, actions and relationships. Knowing this, be intentional!" -
Dr. Cunningham

Now that you can differentiate between motivating and inspiring, how do you manage either? Remember, you can only manage your motivation, not that of others. When employees aren't just engaged but inspired, that's when organizations see real breakthroughs. Inspired employees are far more productive and, in turn, inspire those around them to strive for greater heights (Garton, 2017).

In my thesis, I completed a study on traditional training models' effectiveness in nontraditional training environments. I thought my findings would lead me to a resounding, "No." I thought I would prove that alternative environments called for alternative solutions. Instead, what I found is that the learning environment was secondary.

(if not third-a-rary) to why the learners were there. Participants who needed to know Excel for their job were more likely to attend an Excel class at a church or in a library than those who simply thought it would be cool to learn Excel. So, motivations matter. Now, how do we inspire?

As the gods would have it, my mother, sister, aunts, and five nephews (all around Carter's age) lived in Missouri City, Texas. That's about 60 minutes outside for Houston. Traveling for the job allowed me to see my family. My mom agreed Carter could stay with her while I worked. So, for the next trip, I used a credit card and paid for Carter to accompany me. My plan was to take Carter to my mother's in the morning and pick him up in the evenings. It didn't happen like that. I would work later than expected, or there would be team-building dinners, and Carter would end up spending the night at my mom's. Sometimes he'd stay two or three nights before I got back over there.

But he was with brothers and family and, most importantly, under adult supervision with people I knew. Sounds uneventful, right?

Even as a baby, Carter was never one for naps. He'd lay there but would never sleep. And "never" is not an hyperbole here. The boy never napped. So, it struck me as very odd when, after being at my mom's for three days, I asked my mom, "Where is Carter?" and she said, "I think he's still sleeping." Sleeping? It's 2 pm. I go to the room he was in, and he was lying down, awake but very lethargic. I asked him to sit up, and was taken aback by how woozy he was. I would liken it to a drunken state.

Alarmed, I start trying to identify the problem. "Did you drink something? Take any medicine?" He answered no to all my questions. I asked, "What was the last thing you ate?" He couldn't remember. He's a nine-year-old child, so that was kinda normal. But then I noticed he had on the same clothes from three days ago.

Again, on its own, probably a normal occurrence for a nine year old. "When was your last shower?" He didn't know. Now it's starting to add up. "Cater, when was the last time you ate?" He couldn't remember. I went to the bathroom and turned on the shower. In my normal tone, I told him to take a quick shower then come downstairs so we can go get food.

I went downstairs and saw my mom at her desk and my sister in the kitchen. I calmly asked, "I think Carter is sick. Do either of you know when he last ate?" My sister said, "I called them all down for dinner last night. I don't think Carter came down." My mother said, "These boys are old enough to make sure they eat. I trust them to let me know when they're hungry." I didn't respond to either of them as I turned my gaze to the window.

As I waited in silence, for Carter to come downstairs, I was reminded that I'm a single mother with no real support system.

My mother and sister had no motivation to care for my son or any child for that matter, and, frankly, had not done anything wrong. Knowing them well, it was my fault for blindly expecting them to care for my son as I would have. I'd made the mistake of thinking they'd be inspired to parent differently because all the boys were together. They didn't care about having all the boys together. That was not a motivator for them.

My mother, naturally, is in her own world most hours of the day. So she was completely true to form when she didn't stop and care for a child who wasn't asking for help. My sister prepared food and asked the boys to come eat. She, too, was being true to form by not making a child stop playing video games and eat. So, the current state of my child is on me. I had no one to blame but me. Another motivator emerged: No matter what, Carter's wellbeing comes first. This motivator would later drive most of my life's decisions.

I smiled as I watched Carter bounce downstairs. Simply moving and showering had done him some good. I told my mom I was going to take Carter to get some food. She asked why I was only taking him and not any of the other boys. As I walked out, I said, "They didn't ask to go." I was hottttttt, ya'll!

As we waited for our meals, Carter explained to me how much fun he was having at my mom's house and how he wished he had a brother living with him so he'd always have someone to play with. I gave no real response. He ate his food, and I saw him get more and more back to himself. And I became more and more livid as I thought about him not eating nor bathing for, possibly, days.

My son was alive and healthy. No real harm had been done. I still had a few days left to work on that trip. The situation left me with choices to make. Short term, do I cut the trip short? And, long term, do I continue in this current role? My overarching motivator was to be self-sufficient therefore I could not risk unemployment. The more pressing motivator was to address Carter's well-being. I had to make the best of this situation. Though it was an hour, one-way, I decided I would insist on leaving work on time and would commit to picking Carter up from my mom's every day. There were no other options. I would need to (read: was inspired to) sacrifice my time and comfort for that of my child's health and my family's comfort zones.

I knew Carter would not like the idea of not staying the night at my mom's house. When I told him he'd be going back to the hotel with me, he balked "But mom! This is the only chance I get to spend with them!" When I suggested that we could bring two of the boys with us, order room service, and play in the pool, his face lit up. He was sold! Crisis averted. Kinda.

QUESTION 5: How would you label the following occurrences?

- Carter spending time with the other boys.

  ☐ Motivation   ☐ Inspiration

- Offering room service and time at the pool.

  ☐ Motivation   ☐ Inspiration

I never shared my thoughts and feelings with my mom nor my sister. Like I said, they did nothing wrong. They just didn't do what I would have. I saw a meme that read, "Stop expecting you from other people." I accepted it as that, but I never left Carter there for more than one night again. His well-being was a responsibility, a motivator and an inspiration of mine - not theirs. The adjustment was on me, not them. Understanding the motivations (or lack thereof) and inspirations (or lack thereof) enabled me to adjust accordingly. No harm. No foul. Kinda.

Chapter 5: Real Life Application

"It only takes one person to mobilize a community and inspire change. Even if you don't feel like you have it in you, it's in you. You have to believe in yourself. People will see your vision and passion and follow you."
Teyonah Parris

By now, I think you understand why knowing the difference between motivating and inspiring is important. Personally and professionally, you know to understand what is motivating a person before you try to inspire them. This will save you time, money, resources, and mental energy. Let's look at another real-life scenario and apply what we've learned.

Fast forward a year. By spending half my time in Houston (read: On the company's dime), I was starting to feel some financial relief. My divorce wasn't dramatic, drawn-out, nor traumatic, so I'd moved into a good mental and emotional space.

I was still living check to check, BUT checks were coming in. I could take Carter to McDonald's without any concerns. Embassy Suites has a free happy hour for guests. During the week, I would invite my sister over. She'd bring the boys or pick them up from a stayover, and we'd hang out at the bar for a few hours. When I would stay over a weekend, my sister and I would venture out to a sports bar or a night club. I don't remember what we talked and laughed about, but we talked and laughed!

QUESTION 6: Answer the following.
- Was my sister motivated or inspired to drop off and/or pick up the boys?

  ☐ Motivated   ☐ Inspired

- Was my sister motivated or inspired by the offer of free drinks?

  ☐ Motivated   ☐ Inspired

I'd developed a bit of a social life in Houston. I was casually dating here and there and decided to give online dating a try – in both Richmond and Houston. I wasn't prepared. There should be a "Foolishness ahead" disclaimer on each of those sites. But that, too, is a whole other book. No one I met in Richmond is noteworthy, but I did meet one guy in Houston, Rik. Rik was a young widower and a father of two teenagers. Long story short, Rik and I fell in love. He became the only guy I was seeing, in either city, and I intentionally planned more frequent trips and included weekends so he and I could have that time together. It was a whirlwind romance, to say the least. So much so that after a few months, I met his two kids, and he met Carter. The next month, I requested a transfer to Houston. Carter and I moving to Houston would be a perfect solution for us all. Carter would be around the family more and could grow up being a part of a larger unit. And, Rik and I could begin building a life that didn't involve endless telephone calls and longing for one another. And, in Houston, there were more job opportunities with the bank. My manager approved my request to relocate and Rik and I started house shopping. What started as a curse was turning into a blessing!

QUESTION 7: Answer the following.
- Was being in a whirlwind romance a motivation or an inspiration for me?

   ☐ Motivation   ☐ Inspiration

- Was I motivated or inspired to request being relocated?

   ☐ Motivated   ☐ Inspired

- Was I motivated by or inspired to give Carter an opportunity to be raised with our family?

   ☐ Motivated   ☐ Inspired

About a month later, my manager called to tell me her manager, David, denied my request to have the company cover my relocation expenses. What a blow! I was completely bought into the move and had not even considered the opportunity would be taken from me. My future, literally, was dependent on my moving to Houston. I was devastated at not being able to move to Houston to give Carter the life he wanted and start a life with Rik.

When I shared the news with Rik, he was as wrought as I was. He asked, "What does this mean for us?" Knowing that neither of us desired to be in a long-distance relationship for any real stretch of time, I didn't know how to respond.

In addition to not moving to Houston, my travel there became less frequent as well. The need wasn't there like it had been. This really took a toll on my relationship with Rik. We started speaking less and less about our future and, actually, stopped speaking as much, in general.

On one of my last trips to Houston, I decided to surprise Rik. I called him from the airport, "Guess where I am?" He asked where. "I just landed at Hobby airport. I can be at your front door in an hour!" He paused for an awkwardly long time. Then he said, "Tonight's not good for me," and hung up the phone. I called back. He didn't answer. I called a few times a day, every day I was there. He didn't answer my calls for the remainder of that trip. Though things had been strained, I was heartbroken. You probably already know what happened next. Yep. I went to his house.

QUESTION 8: Answer the following.

- Was Rik motivated or inspired to stop answering my calls?

  ☐ Motivated   ☐ Inspired

- Was I motivated or inspired to show up unannounced?

  ☐ Motivated   ☐ Inspired

Side Note: I would love to hear how these questions are answered by men versus women.

I'd been dealing with Rik in person or on the phone for about six months, so I knew his schedule and his patterns. I knew when he'd be home, when he'd leave for work, when the kids would leave for school and when they'd all return home. I arrived at his house just when he should be leaving for work. Parked across the street, I watched him come outside. He went to the passenger side of his car, opened the door, and turned back towards the house. I got out of the car and started approaching the house. I looked both ways before crossing the street. When I looked back at the house, a woman was coming out the door. And, she was noticeably pregnant. Like, more than six months pregnant! Um, Harpo, who 'dis woman?

In my shock, I didn't stop approaching the house and found myself standing there with them. I lost the fight with my tears and could barely speak,

"So, this is why you're not answering my calls?" She looked at me and asked who I was. I told her I was his girlfriend.

She turned towards him and just stared. She and I stood there, waiting for an explanation. I'd never really been in that kind of love as an adult (yes, even with my husband), so the pain, disappointment, and embarrassment caught me completely off guard. He said to me, "Yes. This is why I haven't answered your calls." I got the answer I came to get. As devastating as it was.

QUESTION 9: Do you think a motivator emerged from this scenario?

☐ Yes   ☐ No

• Why or why not? _____

_____

_____

• If you answered yes, what do you think the new motivator would be?

_____

_____

44

Rik and the woman called me later that day. They explained they'd had a one night stand about eight months prior. She got pregnant and didn't tell him until a few months before my surprise appearance. When he learned I wasn't moving to Houston; he took that as his sign to be involved with the pregnancy and not just the baby. By the time of my surprise visit, they'd started spending time together and would eventually marry.

QUESTION 10: Rik adjusted his behavior with me and with his future wife? He was both motivated and inspired.

• What was Rik's motivation? _____

_____

_____

• What inspired Rik? _____

_____

_____

A month later, the Houston team was displaced, and that site was closed. David, my manager's manager, called me personally and shared that the pending closure was why he declined my request. Ethically, he couldn't allow me to move, knowing I wouldn't have a job a month later. I thanked him for that.

Chapter 6: Conclusion

"Motivation is everything. You can do the work of two people, but you can't be two people. Instead, you have to inspire the next guy down the line and get him to inspire his people."
Lee Iacocca

In this book, you've learned that motivation is an internal drive that usually already exists when you meet a person. Inspiration is an external drive that is only effective if it addresses someone's motivators. Remember when I thought that I'd inspired Carter to do well in school by offering him a trip to McDonald's in exchange for not getting into trouble? Remember how he didn't get into trouble that week? Well, the next week, he was back to being his talkative and independent self. Why? Because he did not have any desire to stop the behaviors that were getting him in trouble. Carter wanted the trip to McDonald's but he knew if we didn't go that week, we'd eventually go – just because. I asked him, "What happens differently that makes you behave well in school?"

He thought about it and said, "I don't know. Some days I care, and some days I don't." That was very transparent and profound coming from a child his age. So, I responded with, "Yeah. I get that. Sometimes, at work, I want to do the work, but then sometimes I don't. But what would happen if I kept getting in trouble for not doing my job?" I'll never forget his response, "You would probably get fired, Mom. But you would just find another job." Whoa! Despite the mental, emotional and financial struggles I was navigating, my son saw me as resilient. He saw me as forever self-sufficient before I saw it. Sniff. Sniff. "And, besides mom, I can't get fired from school for talking." Annnnddddd, we're back.

It was then I realized the kid simply was not motivated to stop talking during class. Realistically, what's the worst that would happen? A note gets sent home to mom? Maybe he'd miss a day or two of recess or a night or two of game playing?

There was no way for me to inspire him because he was not motivated to do what the adults were calling for.

He wanted to play on his high school basketball team. "Cool. You need good grades for that." He wanted to go to the NBA. "Cool. You need to get into college. To get into college, you need good grades." So, grades were never a problem. Though enrolled in Honors and advanced classes, I received regular complaints about Carter's incessant talking and 'disruptive behaviors' throughout his entire academic years. Then, one day, he had no desire to play school ball, and guess what happened?

First, his attendance became sporadic, and then his grades dropped to C's and D's. Not because he wasn't capable of doing better but because he wasn't motivated to do better. And, because he was no longer motivated, I had to adjust my strategies to inspire him based on his new set of motivators.

That's the moral of this story. A person must first be motivated before any of your inspirational strategies can work. And, do not assume you know what motivates a person. Even if you're of the same age, race, and gender, chances are you don't share the same life experiences. Whatever a husband's motivators are to behave a certain way, the wife cannot influence that. The same hold's true in that a manager cannot influence what motivates their employees. Once you understand what a person's motivators are, you can inspire them towards desired outcomes.

This book was designed to be a quick read for the busy professional. If you find that you'd like to have a deeper conversation or you have a team of leaders who could benefit from hearing more on this topic (and others), please do not hesitate to reach out to me.

LaJeanna L. Cunningham, EdD
Dr.Cunningham@thelearningfirm.net
www.llcunningham.com

REFERENCES

Garton, E. (2017, April 25). How to Be an Inspiring Leader. Harvard Business Review. https://hbr.org/2017/04/how-to-be-an-inspiring-leader

Definition of INSPIRE. (n.d.). www.Merriam-Webster.com. Retrieved November 25, 2020, from https://www.merriam-webster.com/dictionary/inspire

Definition of MOTIVATE. (n.d.). www.Merriam-Webster.com. Retrieved November 25, 2020, from https://www.merriam-webster.com/dictionary/motivate

Popomarouis, T. 2019. Entrepreneur leadership. Retrieved from www.entrpreneur.com

Rosen, E. & Sander, U. 2019. Accident Analysis & Prevention, 41(3), 536-542.

Weir, K. 2013. More than a job satisfaction. American Psychological Association, 44(11) 38-39 doi: 10.3102/03465403076073102

www.ingramcontent.com/pod-product-compliance
Lightning Source LLC
LaVergne TN
LVHW051204080426
835508LV00021B/2806